Androphile Pride

G. Scott Graham

"For it is dangerous to attach one's self to the crowd in front,
and so long as each one of us is more willing to trust another
than to judge for himself, we never show any judgement in
the matter of living, but always a blind trust, and a mistake
that has been passed on from hand to hand finally involves
us and works our destruction. It is the example of other
people that is our undoing; let us merely separate ourselves
from the crowd, and we shall be made whole. But as it is,
the populace, defending its own iniquity, pits itself against
reason. And so we see the same thing happening that happens
at the elections, where, when the fickle breeze of popular
favour has shifted, the very same persons who chose the
praetors wonder that those praetors were chosen."
Seneca

CONTENTS

INTRODUCTION

"If everyone is thinking alike, then somebody isn't thinking."
— George S. Patton

THE GAY PREDICAMENT

Let me tell you about Frank.

Frank knows. Somehow, Frank has always known. He's a guy who likes guys. That's about it.

He likes cock. Period.

All would be fine for Frank if it weren't for <u>other</u> people.

Suddenly, there are all these other people who tell Frank WHO HE IS and WHAT HIS LIFE SHOULD LOOK LIKE, all simply because he likes cock.

The ultra-rigid-fear-mongering Christians tell him that he is demon spawn, recruited by an older man and now out to recruit boys to a life that will condemn them to hell. To them, Frank is a fag, more girl than boy, who doesn't know the difference between a flat head and a Phillips head screwdriver.

The so-called gay movement also tells him that he is a fag, encourages him to celebrate his girlishness, and celebrates the fact that he likes cock with a bunch of other guys who like cock (and a few girls who like pussy) while he sips on a screwdriver with breakfast. It is so accepting. It feels like Frank has come home. And it feels like one big party. Frank, who is playfully called Francine, is told he can be himself – in a place where he is loved for who he is – not condemned as demon spawn simply for what he does. Except Frank is not loved for who he is (otherwise his new pals in the LGBTQIAPK community would call him Frank and not Francine). It is not long before Frank discovers that the liberal-leaning gay movement has a long list of views that he needs to not only accept, but also <u>espouse</u> in order to be accepted by the community.

In subtle and not-so-subtle ways, the LGBTQIAPKers indoctrinate Frank. He is *educated* to the fact that now that he acknowledges he's a guy who likes cock, this also means he wants a woman for President. It also means that he likes the Village People. And transgender rights better be on the top of his list right under supporting abortion right up until the moment of delivery. He is now a feminist – and he better be a good one. And he better get some fashion sense – and rather quickly – because he is now the trusted advisor of home decorating tips for all his "straight" friends.

The list goes on and on.

But Frank isn't interested in any of this. He's just interested in men. But that's not enough for today's LGBTQIAPKer community. He is told he needs to embrace himself, and that includes every aspect of their liberal agenda including accepting and promoting drag queens, aberrant gay behavior, and a host of stereotypes.

He is welcomed into the LGBTQIAPKer community or so it seems, and told that now he can be himself, or so it seems. But there is one long caveat: There is a list that defines what this "self" is, and he better embrace it, or that welcome mat will be pulled up. He is told to show his gay pride. Vote this way, he is told. Paint your nails, put on some mascara, prance around in public and make a spectacle of yourself, he is told. And when he doesn't join in lockstep with this world view, he is told he has internalized homophobia.

This is all upsetting to Frank.

To him, who he is sexually attracted to is a small part of who he is. To Frank, there is so much more to him than being gay. But the LGBTQIAPKers tell him that being gay is the beginning and the end at every opportunity, blasting "I Am What I Am" from loudspeakers while a half-intoxicated man dressed up as a woman wearing way too much makeup does a bad job lip-synching the lyrics.

So, Frank finds himself caught! Told by two competing communities that who he has sex with is all that he is. Period. The choice is simple: demon spawn recruiter of young boys, or Francine aka Prance-cine.

Then, one day, Frank discovers the Androphile movement, dripping with testosterone with one seemingly simple membership requirement: You're a guy who likes cock. A guy who knows the difference between a flathead and Phillips head screwdriver. A guy's guy. A man's man. A dude. Embrace your dude-ness. Be yourself. Be a man. Welcome home.

Frank thinks he has found his place. A place where he can be who he is – a guy who likes cock – without making a big deal out of it.

But there is a problem. Actually, there are <u>many</u> problems.

But someone like Frank doesn't care about the problems because he himself is reacting to both competing movements which are at opposite ends of the spectrum. And, because at its core, the roots of the Androphile movement itself are heavily reactionary, the movement seems to "fit" for Frank – responding to all his concerns – to his objections -- to his reactions.

The Androphile Movement appears to be the middle-of-the-road, accept-who-you-are, alternative to the bullshit spewed forth by the LGBTQIAPKers. But it's not.

Because the Androphile Movement had as its source a <u>reaction</u> to the "gay" movement, it was defined in opposition. Think black versus white – there is no room for grey here. And from that opposition-oriented reactive origin emerged reactionary values.

And Frank is now indoctrinated by the Androphile Movement to those values. He is told we don't need gay rights, feminism is crap, etc. Frank learns that just as the "gay" community has a long list of what it means to be "gay", these androphiles also have a list of what is means to be an "androphile." He reads the "bible" of the movement and even learns from the author that if he isn't able to have sex with other men, it's no big deal, just fuck a woman. Look to the initial founder of the Androphile Movement for a role model and you'll walk away with more testosterone-filled stereotypes, not the least of which is to start weight lifting until you have the flexibility of a rhinoceros.

The simple truth is that the early Androphile Movement leaders were just as rigid and judgmental in their perspective as the gay movement has been (and continues to be) in theirs.

This book presents a solution to all of these rigid viewpoints. As such, it augments the Androphile Movement and fosters greater inclusivity. Not inclusivity for one politicized perspective over another, but Inclusivity for the individual, with ample room for individual differences.

Ample room for Frank.

This book also addresses the problem of "internalized homophobia", a term which is no small matter as it has the potential to pollute one's perspective. On one hand, this label – actually an accusation – is used by the LGBTQIAPKers to invalidate and dismiss one's views that are not in line with LGBTQIAPK. And while the LGBTQIAPKers use the term to manipulate its members, the concept of "internalized homophobia" can also be seen as the real genesis of some of the alternative perspectives originally espoused by the androphilia founders.

When you take a deep, hard look at the writings of the early contributors in the Androphile Movement, you will see that its perspectives are driven equally by its own internal homophobia and by an attempt to build an alternative to the pre-ordained identity that the "gay" movement perpetuates. You don't have to look any further than the perspectives on same sex marriage that the early contributors to the Androphile Movement held out, such as: "We don't need same sex marriage." This makes absolutely no sense. Considered simply from an economic perspective, a guy who is in a serious, committed relationship with another guy <u>would</u> want same sex marriage. After all, why the hell should he pay more in taxes than his heterosexual neighbors who are married when he has the same type of relationship but with another guy? Why would he not want the same protections? If these, pry-my-gun-from-my-cold-dead-hands-manly-men were really men, they would be saying "I am not paying extra taxes because you won't recognize my same sex relationship, and if you come on my property to try and get those taxes, I will shoot you." But they don't.

This book expands the Androphile Movement to where it should have been to begin with: an alternative -- not a reaction -- to the gay bullshit rhetoric that guys are fed when they go to their first "gay pride" event. An alternative that is grounded in you figuring out who you really are: not demon spawn, not Prance-cine, not manly Rhino-Frank – you! An alternative that does not ignore the impact of homophobia in the world around us (and actually encourages you to genuinely explore ways you may have internalized some of the world's homophobia), without being injected with gay rhetoric. (One inventory concocted by the LGBTQIAP-Kers actually suggests that if you feel like you are different from other androphiles, but you do not want to join the LGBTQIAPKer community and march in a Gay Pride parage wearing makeup and tight leather shorts, you might have some internalized homophobia).

This book helps you identify the accusations designed to minimize and manipulate you, and explore your authentic true voice, the voice of who you are and not the voice that has mimicked what some author, leader, or social movement is trying to shove down your throat. This book helps you discover and embrace <u>YOU and YOUR androphile identity</u>. As such, you won't find propaganda and edicts in this book. (After all, it's not about MY androphile identity). What you will find are lots of questions for you to ponder and answer. In fact, you would be well-served to get a journal to record your thoughts, reactions, and ideas. Your journal is the real androphile pride book, a book that is about you, your values, your life, your vision, and your identity.

Please note that all this does not mean this book is opinion-free. In fact, it is spewing with my opinions. But the difference between what I will hold out for your consideration and what the "leaders" in the gay and the androphile communities hold out is that I won't pressure you to accept and adopt what I present to you in this book. If you choose to disagree, contest, or ignore any or all of what I outline in the coming chapters, I won't suggest that you are somehow less-than or in any way flawed or screwed up.

Ralph Waldo Emerson said, "To be yourself in a world that is constantly trying to make you something else is the greatest accomplishment." I hope this book helps you to find and be yourself – a true androphile.

G. Scott Graham-Stephens
November 2020

I'M NOT HOMOPHOBIC

I am prepared to be accused of being homophobic or need-ing therapy simply because I wrote a book that is critical of the LGBTQIAPKer community. That's not true. I have been involved in the gay community. In fact, I was out and involved in the gay community when it took great courage to be in the forefront.

Here is a newspaper photo from **February 10, 1988** of Barry Brinson, Ken Williams and myself at a booth at the Florida State Fair, educating those who came to the fair and walked by our booth to the fact that gay men were out and proud in their community:

I was an active member of the Tampa Bay Gay Hotline, a key organizer of gay pride events. I was even so "out" that I was ap-pointed "Minority Affairs Advocate" for the Student Government at the University of South Florida. I was active in the early HIV education and prevention efforts – talk about radical, it was – as I sought to put information in all incoming student's welcome packets about safe sex!

But over time, the gay community was hijacked by subgroups and subcultures. If you didn't agree with the new propaganda put out by the ever inclusive, hyper-liberal gay community, or were in any way critical of the emerging leaders in the community, you were accused of being screwed up in one way or another, and probably so screwed up that you didn't even know that you were screwed up. Classic group-think policed by the "politically correct."

You better be against abortion and in support of a constitutional amendment for women's rights and transgender rights – even though that has absolutely nothing to do with being sexually attracted to another man. If you criticized the sexual promiscuity rampant in the gay community and suggested that monogamy was a better alternative, you were not sex positive and were shaming those who wanted to fuck the world.

And overtime, slowly, emerged the LGBTQIAPKer community.

Most people are surprised that I have been to San Francisco for at a half dozen week-long vacations and have never once been to the gay ghetto nor stepped foot in a gay bar. That's because being gay is not all of who I am. Instead, I have been through Golden Gate Park on a Segway many times, hiked Angel Island, biked across the Golden Gate Bridge, explored the Marin Headlands and even did Tai Chi outdoors. Because that is who I am. I am much more than who I have sex with. I am much more than drag queens, getting drunk, and getting laid. Because at its core, getting laid is not all that being gay is about. There is so much more to life than that.

Note: Throughout most of this book, you will see the term LGBTQIAPK community instead of gay community. And you will see the term androphile instead of homosexual or same sex attraction.

G. Scott Graham-Stephens
January 2021

BULLSHIT

"Believe nothing merely because you have been told it."
—Buddha

THE GAYS, OR AS THEY ARE NOW KNOWN AS: LGBTQIAPK – WTF!

The gay "movement" (now LGBTQIAPK) has changed much in the past 35 years. It has become more inclusive, more encompassing of liberal ideals, and more politically correct. However, group-think has emerged, and any perspective outside the platform of the so-call gay leaders results in those who dare disagree being shamed and branded as being screwed up, "less-than" and flawed", and in need of some sort of therapy to bring them in alignment with the movement.

For most, that branding is the term "internalized homophobia." I know, I know, I used it in the introduction. But I truly despise the term "internalized homophobia." In fact, I don't like the word "homophobia" period! It feels diagnostic. It feels like a label. It feels like an excuse. It feels wounded. It feels weak. It feels like something you need to go to therapy for years in order to resolve.

This branding by the gay movement has been and is the cause of internal conflict within the person—am I really gay if I don't conform?? This is a great place to start the exploration of who you are.

No other social, racial, or ethnic group brands its members in this way. You don't see people struggling with Mexi-phobia, African American-phobia, or Jew-phobia. It is clear to Black people that they are black, Hispanic people that they are Hispanic, etc. They don't struggle with identity, with who they are. Now, that doesn't mean that those communities don't practice group-think, pressuring people in those groups into conformity. They just use terms like "Uncle Tom", or may simply label a person as a "sell out." It is clear that the purpose of these terms (including the newly create RINO label used by Donald Trump) is conformity. They are used with the hopes of creating a critical backlash on those who question or differ from what the so-called norms are for their community. The intent is clear, and the outcome is often certain, direct and powerful. Often the recipients of these labels push back, calling them for what they are: name calling. In fact, those who are labelled often respond with their own criticism of those who are doing the labelling. Rarely do these name-calling labels get any traction outside of a twitter storm or social media meme. Certainly, they get zero traction with those they are lobbed upon. (No Republican Senator who has been labelled a RINO has turned to psychotherapy to resolve their own internally conflicted conservativeness!)

Yet, branding is what happens for many in the androphile community who won't put on makeup, won't refer to their friends as "Mary," won't adopt effeminate mannerisms, and won't participate in other "pro-queer" behavior. They are told that they have unresolved issues to resolve. The only thing more messed up than the pressured group-think around these behaviors and mannerisms is that these behaviors and mannerisms are rooted in stereotypes from the mainstream community!

Can you imagine if Blacks expected other Blacks to adopt the mannerisms of Aunt Jemima, Amos & Andy, or other racist stereotypes? Can you imagine if Blacks expected other Blacks to adopt racist dialects? Of course not. That would be fucked up! These and other systemic racist strategies are instead called out for what they are by people in these communities.

Yet, an androphile daring to call out similar trends in the LGBTQIAPKer community invites condemnation. That's fucked up!

INTERNALIZED HOMOPHOBIA

There are many name-calling labels used to promote conformity to a group. But none of these labels is as clinically accusatory as the term "internalized homophobia." It is nothing more than a group-think strategy to brand those who don't agree with you, and either dismiss them or manipulate them into conformity!

Simply defined, a phobia is a fear. Someone who has acrophobia (fear of heights) experiences extreme anxiety when they are only a little off the ground. It can range from anxiety about being on a step stool or ladder to being on anything but the first floor of the building. These people avoid heights as if their lives depended on it. But they don't hate step stools, hope to burn all wooden ladders, nor plot the destruction of multi-story buildings. They are afraid, not only about falling, but also the sudden stop at the end.

So, is that what homo*phobia* is about? Fear? That's it?

No, the term homo*phobia* as wielded by many LGBTQIAPKers, is about a lot more than fear. It's about bias, prejudice, stereotypes, and of course, hate.

It Makes Sense: It is What We Are Taught

If you are told for years that having sex with people of your same gender is something that will get you a ticket straight to hell, and you buy into that line, then when you do acknowledge your androphilia, you have to resolve that lie – a lie that you have bought completely into over the years.

That's a BIG deal, and not just because you have been sold a bill of goods that is completely false. It is a BIG deal because you have been able to hide in plain sight – to fit in – with those who sold that lie. And now you not only need to come to terms with that lie, but you also need to come to terms with the dumbass who sold you that lie. That second part – the hiding in plain sight part --is the real BIG deal. No other ethnic or racial group has to navigate through this crap. It is clear that Black people are Black, Hispanic people are Hispanic, etc. And for the most part, they are surrounded by others in their community and raised in the same camp.

I remember the first person I told about my sexual attraction to other men, a Catholic Priest at the Catholic Student Union at the University of South Florida. Now, did I make an appointment to talk to this priest? Nope. Did I go up to him after Mass and say, "Hey Padre, got a minute? I have question or two"? Nope. I went to confession. Back then (then was the early 1980s), you had a choice to either kneel in the confessional behind a screen, or to walk around and sit in a chair and make your confession face-to-face. It felt like time had stopped in the small room while I stood behind the screen deciding whether to kneel or walk around and "confess" face to face with a priest I had never met before. "Are you there?" asked the priest. I answered "yes" as I walked around the screen to a sight I will never forget: a 300-pound bald man sitting on a chair that was way too small for his large frame. I sat down and stumbled through my words. I don't remember exactly what I said, but I do remember the response of the priest: "God loves you. God doesn't hate the sinner – but condemns the sin." This was not the first time I had heard this phrase. But it was the first time someone had said it directly to me in the context of my life and my choices.

The rest of the conversation is as clear as crystal in my mind as if it had happened yesterday:

"What do you mean?" I asked already knowing the answer.

"God loves you but not what you do." the priest replied.

"What's that supposed to mean?" I argued.

"It's OK that you are attracted to men, but to act on it is a sin," the priest stated.

"What are you saying? It's OK that I am gay but I can't have sex with another man for the rest of my life? Is that what you are saying?" I asked.

"We all have our crosses to bear," the priest stated in a consoling manner. "Look at me, I am celibate."

Well, I did look at him. Then something snapped.

I stood up, looked at him directly in the eyes, and stated, "First you are a priest. You made a choice to enter the priesthood fully aware of the requirements, one of which is celibacy. I didn't choose to be gay. And second, you are fat and bald, so even if you weren't a priest no one would fuck you anyway."

He just stared at me his eyes wide and mouth open.

I didn't say another word. I just stood up and walked out, never to go back.

Belief or Fact?
People used to believe the earth was flat, and they acted accordingly for fear of falling off the edge. But once they realized the earth is round, their fear was gone, their world was altered by that knowledge – forever altering their behavior. Now apparently – don't ask me why – there are still people around today who believe the earth is flat. Now, if you were raised with that belief, and you are now faced with going on a trip someplace, you have to resolve the conflict between the line you were fed and the fact that you are travelling around the globe.

Or better yet though completely unproven, there are people who believe that vaccines are dangerous and you should never ever get one – so what if there's a measles outbreak! Now you have been fed line for years that vaccines are dangerous, and now you don't want to get the measles. You will need to resolve the conflict between the line you were sold about vaccines and the need for the vaccine, in order to take action and actually get a vaccine.

That's what it is about with same-sex attraction. You have heard something and believed it, and now there is a conflict between what you are experiencing and what you've been told, and you need to resolve it.

It's All About Control

So why the term "homophobia" – and specifically "internal homophobia"? I will tell you why. It's about control. Control by the LGBTQIAPKers. Control over you. A way to dismiss any criticism and dissention. Have an issue with some position espoused by the LGBTQIAPKers? Well, they will say that's because you have some unresolved internal homophobia going on.

So instead of dragging that term around, here's a new one, "buying into the bullshit." It's broader than homophobia. Using the term "homophobia" just addresses the negative values that society spews out.

After all, it is just a group-think strategy – some expectation about conformity that you are fed at one point or another. Like the bullshit line that being gay is demon spawn, so you introduce the guy you have been living with and having sex with for two years as your "roommate" because you don't want to hear "Oh..." and get some judgmental look from a person whose opinion you don't really give a shit about anyways.

"Buying into the bullshit" addresses the negative stuff that "society" tells you about being gay, but it also addresses the normative stuff that the LGBTQIAPKers market to you about your new fabulous "gay" identity. From music, and monogamy, and what your body looks like (I was going to write fitness or health but that is not true – it is really about what your body looks like – which is really about sex), and transgender rights, and what kind of underwear you wear – and everything in between. If you don't buy what they are selling and toe the party line, well then, you are homophobic. That's the bullshit line they sell you to control you and keep you from speaking out. Don't buy it.

STEREOTYPES – THE ROOT OF THIS BULLSHIT

Consider this example: You don't like Paul (I just chose a name), a flamboyant, openly "gay" man who floats into the company Christmas party, calls the other guys "honey", paints his fingernails hot pink, and wears lip gloss. That makes you uncomfortable. (And that is one of the "symptoms" according to more than one clinical assessment, that means you are homophobic).

Let's think about this for a moment. Is the issue that you are at your core somehow uncomfortable with your own sexuality, as those LGBTQIAPKers would have you believe? Or it is more likely that the real issue is that you don't like that Paul confirms every single negative stereotype out there for others at the party, and you don't like that these other people are going to group you in with him. He's a caricature. And if we speak up and call it that and tell him to knock it off, then it's us with the issue. The LGBTQIAPKers tell us that we aren't gay positive. The LGBTQIAPKers tell us we aren't tolerant and that we have internalized homophobia.

That is bullshit.

Why is it that Walt Disney pulled "Song of the South" off the shelves? Because it showed stereotypes about Blacks. Yet you can easily watch "The Birdcage" which shows gay stereotypes that are just as invalid to gays as the black stereotypes in "Song of the South" are to Blacks.

Why are people up in arms about "Little Black Sambo", "Aunt Jemima", or "Mammy"? Because they are degrading.

Yet the "gay community" celebrates a drag queen named "Malestia Child" and appoints her and the man dressed all in leather with a naked boy wearing only a full leather dog mask by his side as marshals for the gay pride parade!

What is going on?

Those People are Not Me. Those People Are Not You.
Those people only represent a very small minority in the "gay" community. Yet, regardless of the fact that they are a small minority, they are held up for us to admire. They are held up for us to emulate. And if we do neither, there is something wrong with us.

Having a negative "reaction" to these stereotypes is spot on. We need to push back. They are not us. We need to take the same attitude toward these people as the Hispanic community does to the images of Mexicans in sombreros lazily taking siestas on sidewalks, full from consuming chile, tacos, and tequila.

The stereotypes are just the tip of the ~~Gay~~ LGBTQIAPK – WTF! Iceberg
The group-think leaders have an entire social program they expect you to buy into. It includes many aspects of the liberal agenda from feminism to climate change, from pro-abortion to rights for trans people. These have absolutely nothing to do with who you fuck, but the LGBTQIAPKers out there would have you think that:

Who you fuck = who you are,

and

who you are = marching lockstep with the liberal agenda.

That's bullshit.

YOU NEED TO KNOW HOW MUCH YOU ARE BUYING IN

Not taking a hard and regular look at how much you are buying into other people's bullshit turns you into a pre-programmed robot of a human being. You are simply allowing your true self to be hijacked by other people's viewpoint. This hijacking is not a once and done process. We drift over time based on the people we surround ourselves with in our lives. We drift over time based on the people we <u>don't</u> surround ourselves with in our lives. The hijacking is subtle. A little bit at a time.

To illustrate this hijacking process, consider this question: if you are a health-conscious runner and <u>love</u> running but surround yourself with couch potatoes who eat cheese doodles but watch re-runs of "Game of Thrones" over and over, guess what you will be doing 5 years from now if not sooner? (Here's a clue: it's not running, even though you <u>love</u> running).

Or, closer to home, you are a country music-loving redneck but you surround yourself with a bunch of disco-loving LGBTQIAP-Kers who paint their nails and watch musicals over and over, guess how you will be 5 years from now if not sooner?

Be your own man, not someone else's.

SO HOW CAN YOU TELL HOW MUCH YOU ARE BUYING IN?

The only way to tell how much you are buying into group-think is to dig deep and examine your values and your beliefs. To get there, you simply follow a two-step process focused first on your feelings, and second on the thoughts behind those feelings. (And you don't need some therapist or counselor to do this).

Step one, look at your feelings in general. You know what they are. And even if you couldn't name them, you know whether they are positive feelings or negative feelings. Take a look at the dominant feelings in your life. Do you feel things like happiness, joy, love and peace? Or, do you feel things like worry, anxiety, sadness, depression, and loneliness? The former is good. The latter is an indication that something is awry in your life. There is a disconnect. That's it, you are done with step one, feelings.

Step two, if the latter is true (you feel things like worry, anxiety, sadness, depression, and loneliness), your task is to figure out what the thoughts are that are hooked to those feelings. To do this, you have to acknowledge what that voice inside your head – the one only you hear – the one that sounds like you – is saying to you. You might have to dig for a while to get to the roots. Don't stop at the first thought that jumps out at you.

To take step 2 further and identify a deeper level of thoughts hooked to your feelings, simply add the word "because" at the end of each thought. Then wait to see what the voice inside your head adds on to the end of this new sentence. At some point, you will run out of reasons for the thought. Then you can look at the last few words you added to determine if the source is primarily driven within you or primarily driven by some outside source.

Here's an example:

> Bob feels a bit depressed. He examines this feeling and uncovers this thought hooked to the feeling of depressed: "I am depressed because I am a slob." He adds another "because" and gets: "I am depressed because I am a slob because I wear wrinkly clothes and no tie." He continues with another because: "I am depressed because I am a slob because I wear wrinkly clothes and no tie, and because other people say you aren't professional if you don't wear a pressed suit and tie."
>
> At this point Bob had exhausted his "because" add-ons. And he can see that the source of this "thought train" is the opinions and assumptions others make about people who don't dress nice and neat. Bob's now in a position to look at whether this value is something he agrees with or not.

Like Bob, if you identify any negative emotions, your task is to slowly drill down to the roots – your values and beliefs. Then you can examine whether these are truly your values or something that you are buying into. Remember you aren't applying this process to your entire life. You are applying this to your androphile focus. As you do this, there are three potential external sources for your "thought trains":

1. Society in general, including your community, neighbors, church, laws,
2. The LGBTQIAPKers, and
3. The androphiles

In the remainder of this chapter, we will take a look at the first two. We'll explore what the androphiles say in the following chapter.

Society

The first of the three potential external sources for your "thought trains", is Society. Society's themes as you explore your negative feelings and thoughts around your androphilia may be: (1) same sex attraction is unnatural, (2) same sex attraction is a sin, (3) same-sex attraction equals molestation of children. (Remember, you are checking out any negatively-focused emotions like worry, anxiety, sadness, depression, and loneliness).

The first theme maintains that you are somehow unnatural, which includes ideas such as you are going to get this disease or that disease, you were not parented well, you are suffering from some sort of psychological trauma, you can be cured, you need therapy, if we allow same sex marriage then people are going to marry goats, you are unable to maintain a relationship, you have mommy issues, get the idea?

The issues with the second theme, that androphilia is a sin, are grounded in quotes from the one holy book or holy writings that this religion and that religion adhere to. Ignoring the fact that there are many of these "the one holy book or writings," the biggest clue is that there is typically a quote (from the book or writings) and a source reference (chapter, verse, page, etc. from "the book"). This serves to do more than attribute or authenticate, but also make the statement seem more important.

The third theme, that same-sex attraction equals molestation of children, adheres to the mythology that you were somehow molested and recruited into the androphile life, and you are now out to recruit others – namely young boys. It reduces same-sex attraction to something akin to drug addiction combined with joining some cult.

LGBTQIAPKers

The second potential external source for your "thought trains" may be the LGBTQIAPKers. Unfortunately, in many ways, living a life that honors your androphilia is like joining a cult, at least as far as the LGBTQIAPKers are concerned. You need to embrace their values, political agenda, and world view. Otherwise, just like their straight society counterparts, they will assert that there is definitely something wrong with you. The LGBTQIAP-Kers want you to be open minded and embrace their world view, and they promise to openly embrace you in return. Disagree, question or criticize them or their values, and you are diagnosed as homophobic on some level and not welcome.

The list of values, political agenda, and world views spouted out by LGBTQIAPKers is as ever growing as their alphabet name. In college in the mid-1980s, I was president of the Gay and Lesbian Coalition, which was at the end, more gay than anything else because all the lesbians hung out at the Womyn's Center (yep, women with a "Y"). There was no agenda other than getting together with other guys for fun things like canoeing, going to the beach, bringing a film to campus, and publishing some information about safe sex (which was hugely controversial). Now look at it—LGBTQIAPK? And it seems with each letter, the rigid political agenda you need to buy into and support got narrower and narrower. There is no theme to watch out for with the LGBTQIAPKers except intolerance for anything other than their way of thinking. And mass marketers have jumped on the bandwagon brainwashing you with everything from pants to vodka to lotion for your balls. The result of this is that many androphiles go back in the closet – at least as far as their values and world views. They stay silent so the rigid left doesn't label them as homophobic and intolerant.

TAKE A LOOK AT YOUR ACTIONS.

There is an old saying that actions speak louder than words (and they are certainly louder than that voice in your head).

Here are some actions for you to look at:

- Do you correct people who assume you are heterosexual? You know the people who ask when you are going to find the "right" girl? Do you respond with "you mean right boy" or do you play along?
- If someone asks if you are "gay" what do you say? Regardless of how you respond, does the person leave with the impression that you are attracted to men or women?
- If you are in a relationship, consider the following:
- How do you introduce yourself and your same-sex partner (or the absence of an opposite sex partner)?
- When you are out at a party, do you dance with your husband or boyfriend?
- What about public displays of affection? Do you hold hands, kiss, say I love you?

What parts of your life are you keeping in the closet so that society (friends, family, church, neighbors, etc.) doesn't find out?

Here are some other actions for you to look at:

- If you hold a political opinion that is different than that held by LGBTQIAPKers, do your LGBTQIAPKer friends know it?
- Do you purchase specific clothes, aftershave, liquor or other items marketed to LGBTQIAPKers in order to fit in?
- If you see someone who is obviously flaunting that they are gay, perpetuating a stereotype, what do you do?
- Do you correct people when they assume that you hold a viewpoint on a societal issue that you don't?

What thoughts, perspectives and ideas are you keeping in the closet so the LGBTQIAPKers don't find out?

Now consider these same situations, but take a look at how you are feeling or what is happening physically when you are in them. Your physical response is even a bigger clue to how much you are buying into the bullshit. If you are dancing with your husband at a heterosexual friend's wedding and your heart is racing and you are feeling sweaty and maybe even a little clammy (all signs of anxiousness), that shows that even though you are acting like you are not buying in, there still is a part of you that buys into the bullshit from society. And if you are hanging out with your LGBTQIAPK friends and you talk about monogamy and fidelity as core components of a committed relationship, and your voice cracks and your mouth is dry and you are a little short of breath (all signs of nervousness), that show that even though you are acting like you are not buying in, there still is a part of you that buys into the bullshit from the LGBTQIAPKers.

If same gender attraction, sex, and relationships are normal, it should feel normal when talking about it or expressing your love. If same gender attraction is no big deal, then it should be no big deal to talk about it even with others who are do not share your sexual orientation.

If your voting record and political views are welcomed with openness and nonjudgement, it should be no big deal to share it with a LGBTQIAPKer.

You probably don't have any issue when telling someone when you are ordering pizza what you like on your pizza and what you don't like. Your heart probably doesn't race nor does your voice crack when you order a pizza with mushrooms and pepperoni, and you specify no anchovies. Because there is not even a small tiny part of you that is even a little worried about what someone else might think of your pizza order, it's no big deal.

Your sexuality should be no big deal. And displays of affection between two androphiles should be no big deal. And your political views should be no big deal. And your critique of walking and talking stereotypes in the LGBTQIAPK community should be no big deal. Just like our jobs, what kind of car we drive, music we listen to, TV shows we watch, beer we drink, and pizza we eat.

If it feels like a big deal – even a little bit – that is something to be vigilantly aware of. Why? Because that could shift your behaviors, and even a little shift over a lifetime means you are wasting part of your life because of other people's bullshit.

It's your job—first and foremost – to sort it out and get your shit together. Then and only then will you be able to move on to looking at the parts of the LGBTQIAPKers that they want you to swallow, and decide whether or not you are going to swallow it.

Check out some of the things that the "Rainbow Project" lists on their website as signs of internal homophobia (https://www.rainbow-project.org/internalised-homophobia):

- *"Feeling you are never good enough.*
- *Engaging in obsessive thinking and/or compulsive behaviours.*
- *Under-achievement or even over-achievement as a bid for acceptance.*
- *Low self esteem, negative body image.*
- *Becoming psychologically abused or abusive or remaining in an abusive relationship.*

- *Attempts to pass as heterosexual, sometimes marrying someone of the other sex to gain social approval or in hope of 'being cured'.*
- *Increased fear and withdrawal from friend and relatives.*
- *Shame or depression; defensiveness; anger or bitterness.*
- *School truancy or dropping out of school. Also, work place absenteeism or reduced productivity.*
- *Continual self-monitoring of one's behaviours, mannerisms, beliefs, and ideas.*
- *Clowning as a way of acting out society's negative stereotypes.*
- *Reluctance to be around or have concern for children for fear of being seen as a paedophile.*
- *Conflicts with the law.*
- *Unsafe sexual practices and other destructive risk-taking behaviours-including risk for HIV and other STIs.*
- *Separating sex and love, or fear of intimacy. Sometimes low or lack of sexual drive or celibacy.*
- *Substance abuse, including drink and drugs.*
- *Thinking about suicide, attempting suicide, death by suicide."*

So basically everyone. Really, is there anyone who has not ever had even one of these signs on this list?

Oh, and check out these other "signs of internal homophobia" according to the folks at the Rainbow Project:

- *"Contempt for the more open or obvious members of the LGBT community.*
- *Contempt for those at earlier stages of the coming out process.*
- *Denial that homophobia, heterosexism, biphobia or sexism are serious social problems.*
- *Contempt for those that are not like ourselves or contempt for those who seem like ourselves. Sometimes distancing by engaging in homophobic behaviours – ridicule, harassment,*

> *verbal or physical attacks on other LGB people.*
> - *Projection of prejudice onto another target group.*
> - *Mistrust and destructive criticism of LGBT community leaders."*

Look over the items in this list again. This list essentially translates into a strategy to control you. Unless you are a good little gay boy and unequivocally embrace every viewpoint, every agenda and every action that the LGBTQIAPKers want, you are suffering from internal homophobia. Mind control. Group-think. Bullshit.

MORE BULLSHIT

"They don't lie to you because the truth will hurt your feelings. They lie to you because the truth might provoke you to make the choices that won't serve their interests."
—Unknown

THE FIRST ANDROPHILE ALTERNATIVE

In 2006, Jack Donovan published "Androphilia: A Manifesto: Rejecting the Gay Identity, Reclaiming Masculinity" under the pseudonym "Jack Malebranche." This book lit a fire under the Androphile Movement. Donovan subsequently published an expanded edition of his book in 2012. Then, according to his website, www.jack-donovan.com, he stated he "pulled Androphilia out of print in 2017, because I followed my own advice and transcended both that identity and that sexuality."
At the time writing my book (January 2021), Donovan's book is indeed absent from Amazon.com, though one can purchase the eBook version from Google Play.

Donovan's manifesto is highly critical of the LGBTQIAPK community. Donovan eloquently outlines many issues that continue to ring true with gay men who find themselves criticized, diagnosed and marginalized because they don't march lockstep with the supposed leaders of the LGBTQIAPK pride movement (the bullshit outlined by me in the previous chapter).

However, after finding validation in Donovan's observations of the LGBTQIAPK community and his solutions to those issues, many who continued to stay connected to Donovan found themselves, in the years since Androphilia's publication, at a new level of bullshit, one grounded in racism, misogyny and hate.

This new level of bullshit was actually the nexus for my writing this book.

In this chapter, we will review Donovan's initial arguments and conclusions as presented in his book, "Androphilia" then survey the current state of bullshit put forth by him.

Powerful Conclusions from the first Androphile Manifesto
Donovan's work had many issues that resonated with gay men, including:

- This great rhyme (I wonder how long it took Donovan to come up with it?) "Men should be defined by what they do, not who they screw. Sex is great, and it's part of life. But it's merely part of life."
- "Men who love men have a place in a world beyond the gay world."
- "I am not gay because the word gay connotes so much more than same-sex desire."
- "One can only have so many cocktail hours and make snide remarks about pop culture for so long before life becomes monotonous."
- "Gay culture celebrates queeniness, but gay porn is almost exclusively a celebration of hypermasculinity."
- "For so many of my peers and their predecessors, actual homosexuality was incidental. Being gay was everything. It wasn't a sexuality; it was a social group. Being gay was freedom rings and a rainbow flag; it was a haircut, a selection of must-see movies and must- buy records and must-go-to events. Gay culture was completely homogeneous, both visually and intellectually. Being gay not only demanded a certain aesthetic, but the acceptance of a set of maudlin sentiments, inside jokes and political ideas."
- Donovan accuses the modern Gay Rights Movement as "an industry unto itself that rakes in millions of dollars and supports thousands of employees overall. The HRC

has a snazzy Washington, D.C., headquarters, and the Gay & Lesbian Alliance Against Defamation throws posh awards ceremonies attended by the Hollywood elite. The Gay Rights Movement has become the Gay Advocacy Industry, and it survives by selling memberships in The Gay Party. Bumper stickers are the new armbands, and they are everywhere."

- "The gay identity, as it is packaged, commodified and sold to the same-sex-inclined, supersedes all other identities. Homosexuality is believed by gays to be a defining characteristic, rendering all other ethnicities, beliefs or allegiances inconsequential."
- "Men who engage in homosexual sex are expected to embrace gay culture and are believed, especially by other homosexuals, to be 'girls on the inside'—no matter how they look and behave, or what their interests may be."
- "While the slogan is 'diversity,' that certainly does not apply to ideological diversity. If anything validates the idea of gay 'ethnicity,' it is not the poorly understood experience of homosexual desire; it is the culture and the near-religious belief system shared by those who choose to identify themselves as gay."
- Donovan predicts that as gay men become more accepted, they will be "assimilated and will feel less of a need to segregate themselves from straight people, and the gay identity will become less important."
- "Gay sensibility is distinct and specialized; it is not directly related to the experience of homosexual desire. Being part of the gay subculture should be a matter of individual preference, not something compulsory or expected of all those who experience same-sex attractions."
- "Effeminate gays still take great pleasure in referring to masculine homos with female pronouns. The real 'internalized homophobia' is the belief that you can't

truly be a man simply because you love other men."
- "The gay community promotes nonjudgmentalism and relativism, only expecting its males to accept their gay identity and find happiness by doing whatever feels good to them at any given time. Gay culture celebrates superficial pursuits like fashion and looking good, but rarely celebrates potential role models who do anything more substantive—unless they're political activists working on behalf of the gay community."
- "Because homosexual men have traditionally been beyond the pale of conventional morality, there are no codes of morality that govern them as a group... ...There's no ideal or model to guide their behavior. Productive male role models are virtually nonexistent. Gay icons are virtually all tortured, self-destructive artists."
- "When homosexuality was illegal, it was necessary for men to have anonymous sex in public toilets, bathhouses, alleys and the like. But the gay community still embraces anonymous, promiscuous sex and fosters a culture of nonjudgmentalism; gays only ask that homos have 'safe' sex. Any suggestion that backrooms, bathhouses and glory holes encourage destructive behavior is answered by cries of homophobia or prudishness."
- "The gay community, because it is a community that grew out of an embrace of alternative sexuality, has an unhealthy, even obsessive relationship with sex. It encourages men to identify themselves not only by who they fuck, but by how they fuck, and we're treated to parades of people who take 'pride' in their sexual fetishes under the auspices of 'diversity.' The gay community makes sexuality a complete lifestyle, instead of merely a part of life."
- "The culture of anything-goes nonjudgmentalism isn't working. Homosexual men, as a group, need some sort of standard that promotes productive rather than de-

structive sexuality, and they have to stop being so afraid to differentiate between the two."

- "Achievement is grossly undervalued in the gay community. The gay community is obsessed with appearance, and status is often 'achieved' via genetic roulette, or by what a gay wears, or how he does his hair, or what personal trainer he sees, or how often he visits a tanning salon. But appearances play a disproportionate role in how gays evaluate each other and how they expect to be evaluated. It skews their value system away from more substantive measures of men. Men aren't held in high regard by other men simply for how they look. Men judge each other based on their skills (what they can do) and on their achievements (what they have done)."

- "Focusing solely on youth and beauty gives men nowhere to go but downhill; it gives them nothing to grow into but the stereotypical 'bitter old queen.' I'll offer that they should be focused on doing something—anything— but wasting their time trying to look like 21-year-old fashion models. Maybe it's enough for some really shallow dimwits to look back on their lives and say "I was really hot." But most people are not going to be perfect tens, and there's a lot more to do in life than be pretty."

- "One of the main reasons I wrote this manifesto, perhaps the primary reason, is that I see so much squandered potential in homosexual males. I see so many intelligent, talented, capable homosexual and bisexual males who are undisciplined, undermotivated and caught up in the superficial distractions that gay culture celebrates."

- "Bitchy gossip is a cornerstone of gay culture. Sometimes, gossip is harmless and in good fun. Often, however, it's mean-spirited, or merely revealing private information for the sake of having something interesting to say... ...It would be refreshing to see androphiles learn how to keep things 'between men.' If a man reveals something intensely private to another man, or has sex with him, the details of the exchange should remain private. They shouldn't become fodder for conversation the next day with anyone who will listen, and they shouldn't be broadcast in a bitchy manner if the two men have a disagreement or go their separate ways. That's fucking tacky, and unmanly to boot."

- "Right now, however, men who love men have no prevailing code, no sense of expectations to live up to at all."

- "What I've suggested here is a loose code of masculine honor, based on values like self-reliance, independence, personal responsibility, integrity, self-respect and respect for other men, that have resonated with males throughout the ages."

- "Character, Not Caricature" (I love this!)

- "This book is an attempt to inspire a new male-oriented subculture, a movement away from gay culture that will develop what I believe to be the natural male potential of homosexual men—the potential in these men that gay culture ignores or actively suppresses."

- "What do you know—really know about homosexuality, about masculinity, and about yourself? Have you perhaps been complacent and allowed others to limit and define you, even as you 'came out' and declared your 'freedom?'"

- "Many homosexual men slip into the gay lifestyle and never look back. They slip into a comfort zone and never really challenge themselves. Being a gay teen might be rough, but being a gay man is easy, especially if you're reasonably good- looking. It's an instant lifestyle. Instant sex. Instant friends. Instant culture. Just add vodka."

Well, what do you think from this handpicked list of quotes from

Donovan's manifesto? Does it make you want to go out and read the entire book?

Unfortunately, from this incredible insightful start, Jack Donovan's subsequent views, evidenced in his blog posts, social media posts, news interviews, speeches and books, took a turn toward more and more bullshit. He has become just as rigid, in the world view he now actively promotes as the LGBTQIAPK community – with the notable difference that his world view had been increasingly associated with misogyny, racism and white supremacy.

THE DOWNWARD SPIRAL TOWARD BULLSHIT

On his website, Jack Donovan has a detailed FAQ section that appears aimed at challenging all the negative information critical of himself that people might come across. Unfortunately, much of the negative conclusions a person would make about Donovan comes from his own writings and posts and behaviors.

For example, Donovan writes on his website, "I don't belong to a political party, I usually don't follow "the news," and I try to avoid commenting on whatever everyone has been told to be upset about on a given day. I am not currently a member of any organization except The American Automobile Association." But when you check out his social media posts (he's not on Twitter, by the way, he's on Parler), you see him writing this (from October 22, 2020):

> *"If you think the two party system is broken (it is) and want something better (sounds great) — three weeks before the election is not the time to decide that. The Libertarian Party is not a viable political entity. If you want to change that, work to make it one."*

And this post (from November 29 2020):

> *"Personal criticism of Joe Biden is boring and stupid. He's a DNC/ Deep State puppet, and unworthy of becoming the same kind of*

specter to people who love freedom that Trump was to the crying genderless slave worms and feckless bugmen. I can't even be mad at Joe Biden. I'm not even sure he is self-aware."

And finally, these words (from January 4 2021) along with a picture of himself in an outside jacuzzi:

"People in blue states waiting in cars outside of fast food restaurants. Me in Idaho enjoying a hotel hot tub after steak frites and negronis out on the town. #redstateflex #redstate #freedomflex Redstateflex should become a trend. Maybe making people who are hating life envious will make them reconsider their foolish ideological and political choices."

I don't know, maybe it's me, but these posts Donovan shared on Parler seem to fly in the face of what he claims on his website.

On his website, Donovan also works to distance himself from The Wolves of Vinland, writing, "I was associated with the Virginia-based folkish heathen organization known as The Wolves of Vinland from approximately

2014-2018. I resigned from the Wolves of Vinland in late 2018. I considered The Wolves to be primarily a private tribal and religious organization. The political and philosophical ideologies of its individual members seemed to vary widely when I was a member." He omits the fact that the Southern Poverty Law Center designated the Wolves of Vinland as a hate group for espousing white nationalist and racist beliefs.

I don't know, maybe it's me, but if you have to write a blog post titled "Why I am not a White Nationalist" or detail on your website why you are not a white nationalist because of the other things you have written or said or participated in, what does that really say about who you are?

A colleague of mine when I worked at the Vermont Department of Corrections, Jack Isselhardt, used to confront offenders who, despite a long history of alcohol or drug related convictions would deny any addiction, used to shrug his shoulders and say this fill-in-the blank rhetorical question:

> "If it walks like a duck, swims like a duck, talks like duck? Then?"

WHAT IS AN ANDROPHILE TO DO?

You may be convinced enough to call yourself an androphile, but now what? How do you figure things out and take the next step? Following Jack Donovan down his rabbit hole is probably not an option. And even if you had a copy of Donovan's androphile manifesto in hand to guide you, you would find little help beyond his proselytizing and fault-finding. Donovan makes a call to action and yet provides no plan of action. In his own words:

> *"If you really want to be a better man, I'm not going to bullshit you. I don't have a system for you to follow or a series of instructional videos to sell. I'm not a therapist and I really don't want to hold your hand or help you work through your feelings about manhood or your father or that guy who made fun of you in junior high school."*

Leaves you kind of hanging doesn't it? He exposes the issue and then walks away. So much for integrity, responsibility and honor.

THE TRUE ANDROPHILE
ALTERNATIVE

"Your success and happiness lie in you."
— Helen Keller

IT'S ABOUT YOU. AND ONLY YOU.

The true androphile alternative is for you to determine who you are – and, ultimately, for you to be proud of who you are. Period.

When you embrace the true androphile alternative, you don't care what the so-called androphile leaders think. When you embrace the true androphile alternative, you don't care what the LGBTQIAPKers think. When you embrace the true androphile alternative, you don't care what I think. All that matters is what <u>you</u> think. Period.

When you embrace the true androphile alternative, you like what you like and it feels normal (meaning no "shoulds") when you talk about those things that you like. The same goes for what you believe – in other words, <u>your</u> values. The same goes for how you present yourself – in other words, your dress, mannerisms, and behaviors.

You may like to do Tough Mudders – not because it is something that a "real man" <u>should</u> do – but because it is a challenge, or it is fun, or it is a fitness goal. You may also like to knit sweaters when not running those Tough Mudders – not because you are embracing some "faggy" side of yourself or because you are embracing what the feminist branch of the LGBTQIAPKers think you should be doing, but because you simply find it a great way to while away the time while you are sitting around.

You may believe that abortion is acceptable because you hold an individual's personal freedom and choice as your highest value. Or you may believe that abortion is equivalent to murder. You may believe that people should choose the bathroom of their internally identified gender because you hold tolerance and acceptance as your highest values. Or you may believe that gender neutral bathrooms have nothing to do with the fact that you like to suck cock.

You may act with stereotypically gay mannerisms: limp wrist, high-pitch voice, pronouncing your "p's", "t's" and "s's" with a hard, crisp tone, prancing around like you have a stick up your ass because that is how gay men <u>should</u> behave. Or you may be as undiscernible from the next guy in terms of the outward expression of your sexuality.

The key to these three areas (likes, beliefs, and behaviors) is discerning who and what you really are from the bullshit that others claim that you should be. The key word here is should. And before diving deep into anything else, it is important that you identify these "shoulds".

GET A JOURNAL

You will need a notebook or journal, and pens or pencils for completing this and the exercises / activities that follow. I highly encourage you to hand write your responses, thoughts, and ideas. You might think that typing them on a computer keyboard will produce the same result as writing, but multiple studies have shown that your brain works differently when we write something by hand. You tend to think more critically, more slowly, and at a deeper level when you write something by hand instead of typing it – and the subject of these activities– you – is indeed worthy of deep analytical, focused, and purposeful thinking. Writing engages your brain differently because you aren't just banging away at the keyboard staring out at the window while your computer auto-corrects what you type and makes every letter neat and pretty. Writing in a journal is primarily a one-shot deal that concurrently engages your cognitive, visual, and motor functions so that you interact with the letters you are writing and therefore the words you are recording in a completely different way. These words are expressions of your ideas so you actually think differently. You have probably heard the term "emotional intelligence" before. Writing by hand (versus keyboarding) actually enhances your emotional intelligence. And I agree with Jim Rohn. Jim Rohn suggests getting a nice journal in which to record your thoughts and activities. The work you are doing can be challenging, insightful, and inspiring, and worthy of something more than some lined paper you got at the office supply store. You are writing about a very important topic after all: you. And the areas you are exploring in your topic – the core of who you are, what you believe, and how you see yourself in this world are worthy of a well-made, quality bound container that you can review from time to time. You are, after all, building your personal life road map.

Top Three Resources for Getting a Journal

1. http://blog.paperblanks.com/2011/11/buying-a-journal/
2. https://www.lifehack.org/articles/communication/these-8-good-things-will-happen-when-you-start-writing-diaries.html
3. https://spaceandtime.com.au/5-tips-choose-diary-thats-right-for-you/

EXERCISE: IDENTIFYING THE "SHOULDS" IN YOUR LIFE

For most people, their "shoulds" are so permeated into their life that it is difficult to identify, let alone evaluate and codify them. You are best served in your efforts to root these out by having some organizational scheme – a plan of attack. Sure, you could just open your journal and write the word "Shoulds" at the top of the first page and go from there, but you will only identify the "should" that are foremost at the top of your mind and the most problematic in your life. You can hack this issue by first identifying the sources of your "shoulds" and then going source by source and listing out the "shoulds" that those sources have communicated to you over the years.

Take your time with this exercise. Give yourself permission to take things slow and with consideration. The goal here is to not miss any aspect of the "operating system" that sometimes blatantly, but oftentimes subtly, guides your actions, thoughts, and emotions.

Get out your journal and make a list of all the sources for your shoulds. Write the word "Sources" at the top of the page. Below that, write the words "Life Areas." Your goal is here is to divide your "shoulds" into broad categories that all add up to 100%. Possible life areas include: family, friends, work, religion, your tribe, community, neighbors and even politicians. You might even list social media or bloggers. Keep the perspective broad at this point. (*Note: as the purpose of this book is to help you forge a path as a man who likes to have sex with other men, be sure to include the LGBTQIAPKers, liberals, feminists, and other flag-wavers out there*).

The next step is to dive deeper into each of the life areas you identified. To accomplish that, simply write a life area on separate page and list the specific person or persons that fall under each area. The more specific you are, the better. However, you don't want to be specific just because you can. For example, your parents may have been united in their efforts, direct or indirect, to imbue you with certain values. In this case you can simply list parents, and not each parent individually. But maybe one parent sent you stronger messages while you were in your youth of how you should or should not be in the world. In this case, you might want to list each parent separately. Make an effort to be as specific as you can with these sources. If you have the LGBTQIAP-Kers for example as a life area, you are better served being more specific than "gay leaders" during your deep dive. After all, the shoulds peddled by Jack Donovan, gay "saint" Harvey Milk (both the real and movie version, which are different) and even Xavier Bettel (he's the Prime Minister of Luxembourg), are each different. The more specific you are, the better your results will be.

In your effort to be specific, strive to write out each item as a sentence. Avoid one-word answers. "Finish things that you start" or "Don't cheat on your spouse" could both be replaced with "commitment" for example, but a sentence provides a much clearer meaning than a single word.

Now that you have identified specific sources in each life area, you are ready to identify the "shoulds" that each of these sources have communicated to you in one way or another. Before you move on to this part of this exercise, take a moment and survey your life areas and the sources under each of those areas one last time to make sure you haven't overlooked an area, a specific individual, or other source.

For this step, take each specific source that you have identified and list under that source all the "shoulds" that the specific source communicated to you. Don't edit or omit anything. In other words, include in the list not only the "shoulds" you currently adhere to, but also include those that no longer appear to guide your actions, thoughts and emotions. Even include those "shoulds" that you discounted from the first time you were exposed to them. This will serve you well by showing the greater context for that person in your life. In other words, if you only list the "shoulds" that you currently seem to buy into and not the ones that you decided from the onset were bullshit, plus the ones you decided were bullshit after trying them out for a period of time, then it will look like 100% of the views peddled by this person were 100% applicable to you. If on the other hand, you list as many of their peddled perspectives as you can, you might find there was only one that you have bought into. that would leave you with some grist to ponder – why that one instead of all the others.

Here's a quick example from when I journaled this process myself. I remember Father Bob. When I was in the eighth grade, Father Bob came in to meet with all the boys for a number of classes on sex education (I know, I know, my eyes are rolling too as I write this example out for you). Now Father Bob was cool. He was younger, rode a motor cycle, and really made an effort to connect with young people. One of the topics he broached with us boys was masturbation – a word I was unfamiliar with at the time, although it was an activity in which I was making an almost daily effort to build competence. I was in shock -- mouth open, eyes wide -- when Father Bob told us that masturbation would not only ruin our life on earth, but would also surely align us on a path to hell for life after death. I asked him during the class (which should be no surprise to you, the reader, after my coming-out-in-confession story, "How can something that feels so good be so bad if you do it every day?" Now, if I had any sense about me at all, I would have looked around at the other boys in the class with their heads lowered and their eyes transfixed on the ground directly in front of their chairs. But I didn't take any notice until every single boy stopped looking at the ground and stared at me after Father Bob responded to my question, not with an answer but with another question: "Do you masturbate every day?" After what felt like 10 hours of silence, I replied in a cracked timid voice "No." To which Father Bob, replied, "Good, you don't want to commit that sin."

Father Bob had a made a strong case for "You should not masturbate." And that was on my list.

Six months after that class, Father Bob gave me another should, although indirect: "You should follow God's rules when they are convenient for you", as he rode off into the sunset on his motorcycle with one of the nuns in the convent next door.

Top Three Resources for Learning about the "Shoulds"
1. https://www.theauthenticpath.com/25-shoulds-you-should-avoid-in-your-life
2. https://www.psychologytoday.com/us/blog/fixing-families/202002/driven-too-many-shoulds-how-reclaim-your-life
3. https://www.verywellmind.com/should-statements-2584193

EXERCISE: YOUR A, B, CS AND DS - EVALUATE THE SHOULDS IN YOUR LIFE

Now that you have a thorough list, it is time to take stock of how much of a driver each "should" is in your life. Your first step is to assess just that. Go through your list, and for each "should" write one or more letters next to each one. Those letters are: "A", "B", "C" and "D". An "A" means you agree with the "should." "B" means you think the "should" is bullshit. "C" means that you act, think, and feel in a way that is consistent with the "should". The "D" means the "should" is in some way or another a driver in your life.

You may benefit, in a later part of this evaluation, from writing at least the "Cs" and the "Ds" in different colors.

The "As" and "Bs" require little explanation, except that beyond that you either agree with a "should" or you don't, you actually might be neutral. You might choose not to put either letter next to an item on your list. An "A" or "B" designation are, however, mutually exclusive. You might review an item and think to yourself, "Well, this is bullshit but I still do it, so I guess on some level I agree with it." The "C" addresses this issue.

The "C" is for consistency in your actions, thoughts and feelings are with the "should" you are evaluating. The consistency label is really identifying how much you are aligned with the "should". This is not necessarily about living your life in some consistent way based on a value – for example, a person might evaluate the sentence from the example used earlier: "Don't cheat on your spouse". They may label this with an "A" and they may be decided to be monogamous with their husband/partner/spouse because of this and that is the ideal they strive for. Another person may evaluate another sentence, for example, "you should not have sex with another guy" with a "B" and indeed they may be sexually active but he still finds himself, after each sexual encounter, feeling guilty about what he has done, indicating on some level that his thinking and feelings are consistent with that "should", even though his behavior is not.

A good indication of thoughts and feelings that indicate some consistency with a "should" can be found with thoughts that may criticize yourself as well as emotions like guilt and remorse – you know negative thoughts and feelings.

"D" is similar to "C" in that you are assessing how you interface with a "should." Whereas "C" is assessing how reliable that should is in your life, "D" is about strength and motivation. And just like "C" a "D" label may be accompanied by "A" (agree) or "B" (bullshit).

Now that you have some orientation to the labels take a few moments and go through your list. Unlike the previous exercise, you want to go through this process **<u>fast</u>**. Jot down your initial reaction then quickly move on to the next item. This is not a process of endless debate and grappling to label each item. Zip through it.

Once you have gone through and labelled your "shoulds" (again this should only take a few moments), go quickly through your list again and rate your "Cs" and "Ds". They should be easy to find if you used different color pens for your labels. Rate each "C" and "D" only on a 1-10 scale (1 is low, 10 is high). If you have low consistency with a "should" mark it with a 1 (and high consistency with a 10). Similarly, if a "should" you labelled with a "D" is not much of a driver, rate it a 1 or a 2 (and a "should" that is a huge driver in your life, mark a 9 or 10).

As when you labelled each "should" earlier in the exercise, you want to number those items labelled with a "C" or a "D" quickly. Zip right thru the list.

Top Three Resources for Evaluating the "Shoulds"
1. https://www.restoredhopecounselingservices.com/blog/2020/4/23/releasing-the-shoulds-freeing-yourself-of-impossibly-high-standards-so-you-can-live
2. https://www.lifehack.org/articles/lifestyle/how-find-your-lifes-purpose-and-make-yourself-better-person.html
3. https://mariashriver.com/how-to-eliminate-the-shoulds-from-your-life/

EXERCISE: AH-HA! AND UH-OH! ONE

As you have probably already surmised, this chapter is filled with a series of exercises. Each exercise is sequential – meaning do them in order – they build on each other. There are three types of exercises – open, evaluative and reflective. Open exercises are like essay questions – I give you a prompt, and your answer – short or long or in the middle -- is up to you. The exercise can also include list making. The first exercise you completed is an open exercise.

The second type of exercise is one where I ask you to evaluate your answer or answers. The second activity you did is an example of this. As in the last exercise, these exercises typically use a rating scale and ask you to evaluate the impact of one thing or another, or rank your answers.

The third type of journaling activity is reflective. This journal work asks you to consider your responses to previous exercises and to record your awareness, your insights, and your conclusions. You will see these exercises peppered throughout this section of the book, identified by the title, "Ah-ha! and Uh-oh!" I've endeavored to keep these as non-touchy-feely as possible. Partly because I am not a touchy-feeling kind of guy, but mainly because as a coach and counselor, I don't see much value in overly creative writing assignments. As a coach I often ask executives with whom I collaborate, to simply record the week's "moral of the story" in their journal rather than some long, free flowing hundred-plus word tome. It is just not worth it in the long run. They are much better served having 52 "morals of the story" that they can quickly and easily access and review then having pages and pages to read through, decipher and apply to their life.

Through "Ah-ha! and Uh-oh!" journaling I want to challenge you to do something similar. And your first reflection using this technique focuses on the first two exercises you completed.

(Each of these exercises are the ultimate product of your efforts, by the way. So, be diligent and committed in your efforts. Give yourself ample time to reflect. That means simply giving yourself a day or two to think about what you recorded in an open or evaluative exercise. You may find benefit to sitting down in a quiet space to think, but this is absolutely not necessary. You can easily do this work while you are driving to work, taking a shower, or brushing your teeth. The important thing is to answer the questions, "So what?" and "Now what?").

To help you organize your thoughts I suggest you focus both on your positive insights and negative insights. Positive insights (the Ah-has) are those discoveries you made in the process. The insights that you see as critical to remember. The conclusions that you see are important to guide you in the future.

Negative insights (the Uh-ohs) are those discoveries you made which reflect the boundaries of where you don't want to be in your life. They may show internal conflicts, or they may reflect lack of alignment between the person you see yourself as and the person you are.

One last nuance to consider as you use your journal. Include all of your insights, even if it is something you already know about yourself. Both Ah-has and Uh-ohs may be new or they may be old. They may be familiar friends or enemies to you. You may be thinking something like, "Yeah, yeah, I know this already." Record it in your journal anyway. In fact, you might want to designate these with a star or some other symbol as they may indicate a stuck point that you have difficulty working through.

In all of this, you need to be clear on what stuff you might buy into, but you also need to be clear on your own direction and where you want to go.

Take some time now to write down your insights around the "shoulds" that are in your life. Look for patterns. Ask yourself the questions you wouldn't let anyone ask you. Explore the benefits and costs of the influences as well as the choices related to each.

And don't ignore your feelings. If something bugs you and you don't know why, just write "________________________________ bugs me and I don't know why."

Use bullet points for each insight you have from the first two exercises.

Make sure you have finished this before you move on to the next exercise. Once you finish all the exercises, you will tap into your Ah-has and Uh-ohs to formulate a plan for your next steps. If you return to this after you do the exercises, your insights will be diluted from the other activities or seem smaller because of the passage of time.

Top Three Resources for the Ah-has and Uh-ohs
1. https://journaledlife.com/reflective-journaling/
2. https://www.holstee.com/blogs/mindful-matter/self-reflection-101-what-is-self-reflection-why-is-reflection-important-and-how-to-reflect
3. https://penzu.com/how-to-write-a-reflective-journal

EXERCISE: YOUR PERFECT LIFE

So many people describe their life based on other people's terms and ideals. These people continue on their path not aware that the life they are living is not truly a life of their own choosing. For some, a tragic event (loss of a loved one, accident, illness, etc.) or a life milestone (turning 40 or 50, retirement, divorce) wakes them up. Others just ignore this until they reach an old age filled with regrets.

Don't let this happen to you. What does your perfect life look like? What would it look like if you lived your life like you wanted to live it without the pressure of conformity from all the people who "should on you?"

This exercise strives to get at your vision for your life. It is a free-form question which asks you to use your imagination and start from scratch with no limitations. People often find it easier to imagine their life at some point in the future, and you are welcome to use this strategy if it seems helpful.

The key quality to focus on for this question is PERFECT. Note that I didn't say realistic. I didn't say if you can. Or if you can afford it. Use your imagination and go into as much detail as possible. If your perfect life has you living on a beach and drinking margaritas, but you don't make enough money to buy beach front property, and you have a problematic sun-triggered skin condition, ignore these limitations. Blueprint your perfect beach life.

The goal of this exercise is to really get to your core values (which you will do in the following exercise).

You may find it helpful to tackle this from two perspectives: your life overall, and a perfect day or even week. Most people's initial response to writing about their perfect life is to focus on possessions and vacations. When they attempt to articulate their perfect life, they write about a life that has a nice house, a nice car, and travelling to far off lands. It is hard to discern what your values are (the primary purpose of this exercise) when the only data you have on which to build conclusions is a brand of automobile or vacation home. That's not to say that "things" don't give you a clue as to your values. There used to be a TV sitcom called "Green Acres" where the wife says: "New York is where I'd rather stay; I get allergic smelling hay; I just adore a penthouse view; dah-ling I love you but give me Park Avenue." Meanwhile, her husband says: "Green acres is the place for me; farm livin' is the life for me; land spreadin' out so far and wide; keep Manhattan, just give me that countryside." Their values, reflected by their lifestyle and evidenced by their possessions, provided the comedic grist for the show. You may find that a lot of the "things" you want to own in your perfect life do reflect a certain lifestyle and specific values.

But you may need to dig deeper to explore your perfect day or even week. This second perspective will prompt you to think more about the actions you take than the things you have. You might think this would avoid the cloudy values issue created by "possession" and accumulation thinking, but there is a trap with the perfect day also. You may find that your perfect day is still vacation or spa oriented. You know, you get up and you have caviar breakfast followed by a massage, then tanning at the pool until lunch when you have lobster followed by a massage, then tennis lessons, then dinner at the country club. If so, try to imagine a time when the novelty of all of this wears off. Sometimes it is helpful to imagine a perfect life in which you have a comfortable life-sustaining income and don't have to work, but you aren't a multi-billionaire who has enough money to buy a small country. The idea here it to identify your typical day and typical week, with activities that are sustainable, repeatable, enduring and fulfilling.

Alternative exercise: Your most feared obituary
Some people have trouble imagining their perfect life. For them it is too forward-focused, or it may be that their mind just doesn't seem to work that way. They can't imagine their best.

The alternative for these folks is to imagine their worst. Some people have no trouble identifying the worst. If this sounds like you, consider writing your most feared obituary. Then, if you have done a really good job at it, your perfect life is the <u>exact</u> opposite of the life you described in your obituary. If your most feared obituary was that you spent all of your time at work making money, went through a string of marriages, and died alone, you might extrapolate that your perfect life is one where you spend time with family, invest in your relationship so it withstands the test of time and bounces back from the vicissitudes of life, and have a rich cadre of friends who are there for you and supporting you at the time of your death.

Key areas to consider
Regardless of which strategy to take to explore your perfect life, be sure and address the following:

> Relationships: Who are they, why do they matter, what are they like? How do you think you will meet (unless you have met already) your life companion / spouse / partner / husband? And what do you call him – speaking of labels – how do you introduce him to others? Do you wear a wedding / commitment band on your left hand?

> Spirituality: What is your connection, what gives you hope, what gives you faith?

> Physical: How's your body, what do you eat, drink, smoke, exercise?

Recreation & Play: What about sports and leisure, are you a chess master? What do you do for fun? Adventure? Where do you vacation? How do you vacation? Do you stay in only 5-star hotels, or are you more of a hostel kind-of person?

Community: Community could be many things, not just where you might live.

Service: Are you doing things to help others, volunteering

Money: How much money is enough money? What would you buy, things or experiences? What kind of things? What kind of experiences?

Work: Think broader than your career. What kind of employer do you have? What is your work environment like? Do you have a long commute? Do you work from home? Wear a uniform?

Personal Development: Learning, knowledge, new skills? How are you growing personally and professionally?

Creativity: Personal expression. Do you like to do wood working, home improvement, making or playing music, chainsaw art, painting pictures, etc.?

Love (both plutonic and romantic): What does this look like – are you connected or not connect, and in what ways?

Sex: How do you get laid? How do you meet people?

Friends: Do you have a lot of friends. Or small network but close intimate friendships? Mainly superficial friends? What is your connection to others and how do you connect? What do you do together? Hike? Bike? Play chess?

Children: Is raising children important to you?

Family: Some people are big into family events. They even attend school plays, birthdays, and vacation together as a group.

Home / Neighborhood: What kind of house do you live in?

A big home, a tiny home? In a suburb? In the woods off the grid? In the north? In the south?

Name Your Own: If I completely missed a category or a nuance of a category, please email me and I will for sure add it!

As you probably have discerned from these categories, this is not a 15-minute exercise. As a coach, I have had clients who spent an hour on each of the categories, writing in great detail about their perfect life.

Your Most Feared Obituary Part 2:

If you chose to write out your worst obituary, take a moment and spin out the positive flip side. Identify the things that are important to you. It can be a list. You don't have to write out your "perfect / best" obituary. But for each item in the list at least write a sentence that expands and clarifies your thinking. This may prompt some deeper thinking. Go through each of the categories above and make sure that you have at least a paragraph for each.

A Cautionary Suggestion: Dive Deep!

You may be tempted to stop at the first few words that come to mind. Persevering in these perfect life exercises will come with a big reward: clear values. Crystal clear values. That is the goal of these questions. And if you stop on a general broad description, you won't get the clarity to know whether you are following your own path or someone else's.

Dive deeper than the words that typically get thrown around when people describe their life. Words like "happy" or "successful" or "accomplished". Even more specific words and phrases like "live a sustainable lifestyle" can be deepened. Consider what a sustainable lifestyle could look like and mean. Does it mean you are vegetarian? Live in a tiny home? Live in a yurt? Grow your own food? Are you canning the food your grow? If you like to drink hard cider, does that mean you have an apple orchard and make your own booze? Is your house solar? Are you off the grid? Do you make your own clothes? Do you heat your home only with wood heat? Only buy your clothes from the second-hand clothing store? Never drive a car – only get around via bike or horse or walking? As you can see, even a phrase like "live a sustainable life" has different interpretations and different boundaries. Your task it to identify the boundaries for each phrase so it is clearly, distinctly and uniquely you.

Your Perfect Life Follow up A

There is no alternative for this exercise. To do this, print out or make a copy of what you have written. If you have been diligent about your efforts while writing out your perfect life, including the categories exercise, you have a document that is full and complete. It is loaded with details from which to identify your core values, the key point of the perfect life exercise. There are two steps to complete: First, identify any "shoulds" that have somehow weaseled their way into your vision; and second, identify patterns, themes, and values that are clear in your vision.

To identify the "shoulds", go through what you have written and, using a highlighter or colored pen or pencil, circle everything that could be a "should". What you are looking for are concepts that may reflect a buy-in, however small, on your part into other people's bullshit. Maybe your parents always wanted you to be a doctor (maybe you even come from a family of doctors) and pushed you to take this class or that class, which set your trajectory to be a doctor, and you are. Maybe you were raised in a rural area and you never ever have been more than 50 miles from your hometown, and your story about people who live in the city is negative. You may even have a fear of going to a city – a place you see as filled with crime, subways, congestion, small spaces, pollution, and rats. I am not suggesting that you buy into these things, or that it is somehow wrong for you to love to be in the profession that you parents wanted for you. You may love being a doctor. You may love living in the country. The goal here is awareness: You are aware of the origin of these pieces of the puzzle of who you are. Knowing the origin of these pieces of your personal puzzle can be quite empowering.

To identify the patterns, themes and values, go through what you have written, and using a different colored pen or pencil than what you used for the "shoulds", write the names of the patterns, themes or values you identify. Maybe you notice a pattern that you are with other people, or you notice a pattern that you are solitary. Maybe you see a theme of physical exercise, or that you exercise because you have to – a "should". Or family and children may be a clear value that emerges from your review, or your value is being single or in a couple that is without children). Take the time to write out your patterns, themes, and values as a single list.

Your Perfect Life Follow up B – Rank your list
Now you are ready to evaluate your list. Simply go through the list you made and put a number starting at #1, and then continuing on for each item in terms of its importance to YOU. Do this quickly. If you are stuck with a tie, force yourself to make an efficient decision and move on.

Save this list. It is the essential harvest of the work you have been laboring through around your perfect life.

Top Three Resources for Your Perfect Life
1. https://medium.com/thrive-global/this-is-why-having-a-vision-matters-5cbe65f13270
2. https://www.jackcanfield.com/blog/how-to-create-an-empowering-vision-book/
3. https://www.earlytorise.com/ultimate-guide-creating-a-life-vision/

EXERCISE: AH-HA! AND UH-OH! TWO

Reflect on your Perfect Life Exercise. What insights and conclusions can you make? Was it easy or difficult? Or were there parts that seemed easy and others that seems difficult? What did you learn? What issues did you see creep in? How was it helpful?

Remember, the Ah-has are those positive discoveries you made in the process. The critical insights and conclusion that you want to guide you in the future. The Uh-ohs are those negative discoveries you made in the process. The conflicts and direction that you don't want to have in your future.

Be sure to write at least 15 minutes in each area.

EXERCISE– WHO ARE YOU?

With this exercise, your goal is to come up with a list of terms that you would use to describe yourself. Just like the previous exercises, your efforts are most fruitful when you dive deep beyond the broad, beyond the general, and beyond the obvious. The first term most people default to is their profession. You know, "doctor", "teacher", "policeman". You are more than your career. Aren't you?

The second term most people default to is some recreational activity. Examples of this include "golfer", "hunter", "fisherman." Think of those plaques and plastic trophies you see for sale that have a list of terms after "World's Greatest:"

You are more than your hobby or past time or fan club, aren't you?

Focus on NOUNS and not ADJECTIVES (adjectives are in another section). The easy way to get going with this exercise is to sit down and fill in this sentence: "I am a ______________________________."

Come up with at least fifty words that describe you. Now, as you can already imagine, the first 10 will be easy, and each 10 after that will be increasingly difficult. Persist and be tenacious with this exercise, ever when it gets hard. That's the point of the exercise – to push you to explore deeply who you are.

This is not a reporting activity, It is a thinking activity. (If 50 come easy for you, don't stop there, shoot for 75). Strive to get to the point where you think to yourself, "this is silly, I can't think of anymore", then come up with 5 more!

You may find it helpful to tackle this thinking in one sitting. Or you might have to spread it out over days, carrying a pocket notebook to jot down the nouns that describe you when they come to the forefront of your mind.

Here's a list to get you going:

Nouns that describe career, profession or avocation: musician, soldier, entrepreneur, life coach, engineer, dancer, logger, electrician, astronaut, doctor, plumber, firefighter, painter, carpenter, photographer, etc.

Nouns that describe a credential: psychologist, QuickBooks pro advisor, CPA, EMT, X-certified person

Nouns that describe an interest: Disneyphile, audiophile, trekker

Nouns that describe activities: half-marathoner, hiker, swimmer, runner, hunter, meditator

Nouns that describe emotions and behaviors: hater, lover, worrier, murderer, rescuer, procrastinator, worry-wart, hotdog, coward, adventurer, dilettante, scaredy-cat, etc.

Nouns that describe accomplishments: college graduate, distinguished toastmaster, tough mudder

Nouns that describe some sort of membership in something: Rotarian, Elk

Nouns that describe relationships: mom, dad, father

Nouns that describe political viewpoints: democrat, liberal, republican, independent, libertarian, conservative

Nouns the describe religious views: Christian, Muslim, Buddhist, atheist, Hindu, Mormon, agnostic

Nouns that describe your gender: male, female, and for those who have bought into the politically correct bullshit, "non-binary"

Note that some words can be both a career and a "hobby". Someone could say "I am a musician", and that could mean that is how they make money, or that could mean that is what they do for fun. (You usually hear someone add the word "professional" before musician in order to emphasize that they make money from playing music – not that those who don't make money from music are unprofessional.). The same is true for certifications or licensure. (Someone can be an EMT but not work as an EMT, where EMT describes their credential.) Don't worry about it. Just make a list!

Who are You? Follow up B – Rank your list. Twice.
Now that you have a list of at least 50 nouns, it is time to rank them. You will need two different colored pens – or you might choose to make two copies of your list. Your first ranking is made in consideration of how you are now. Today. Strive to be accurate and reflect things as they really are, not how you want them to be.

Your second ranking is made in consideration of how you want them to be. How you would like to be. In the future.

Top Three Resources for Who Are You?
1. https://tinybuddha.com/blog/5-questions-discover-who-you-are-and-what-will-make-you-happy/
2. https://thriveglobal.com/stories/thc-art-of-exploring-yourself/
3. https://ideapod.com/who-am-i-the-answer-to-lifes-most-defining-question/

EXERCISE: AH-HA! AND UH-OH! THREE

Reflect on your Who are You? Exercise. What insights and conclusions can you make? Where did the rankings for today and the rankings for the future intersect? Were there rankings on one list that were close to rankings on the other list? For example, number 18 on your ranking for today was number 20 on your ranking for the future. Where did they diverge? Were there rankings that were from the extremeness that swapped? For example, an item near the end of your ranking for today is near the top of your ranking for the future (or vis versa). Write for at least 10 minutes for the Ah-has, and 10 minutes for the Uh-ohs. You can simply make bullet points. You aren't writing poetry. Your insights are for you and need to only be easily recorded and easily accessible.

EXERCISE– WHAT ARE YOUR QUALITIES?

The previous exercise foreshadowed that an adjective activity was forthcoming. And here it is. In this exercise you are simply filling in a blank: "I am a _______________________ guy" or "I am a _______________________ human being" or "I am a _______________________ person."

You might be tempted to just grab your list of nouns from the previous activity and come up with one quality that describes each word. That would be a good start, but avoid just a single descriptor for each word or category. Striving for a minimum of 5 qualities for each noun is a better goal. And like the previous exercises, be diligent of those over-used, generic, and worthless terms (meaning they won't really spell out a path for you) such as "good", "happy", "skilled", etc.

It may be easier for you to consider how other people view you. Simply insert "Other people say..." before each of the filling the blanks above ("People say I am a _______________________ person."). Think of the things about which compliment you.

Strive for 200 qualities, and don't worry about duplicates.

Here's some words to get you going:

- adaptable
- adroit

- adventurous
- affectionate
- ambitious
- amiable
- bold
- clever
- compassionate
- considerate
- courageous
- courteous
- creative
- diligent
- empathetic
- easy-going
- exuberant
- friendly
- funny
- frank
- generous
- genuine
- gregarious
- hard-working
- honest
- imaginative
- impartial
- intuitive
- inventive
- kind
- methodical
- open
- passionate
- persistent
- philosophical
- polite
- practical
- quiet

- rational
- reliable
- resourceful
- serious
- sensible
- silly
- sincere
- spiritual
- sympathetic
- tenacious
- unassuming
- trustworthy
- witty

What are your qualities? Follow up – Rank this list too. Twice.
Now that you have a list of adjectives, it is time to rank them just like you did the nouns. As with the previous exercise, you will need two different colored pens or pencils – or you might choose to make two copies of your list. Your first ranking is made considering how you are now. Today. Strive to be accurate and reflect things as they really are – not how you want them to be.

Your second ranking is made in consideration of how you want them to be, how you would like to be in the future.

Top Three Resources for Qualities
1. https://owlcation.com/humanities/how-to-describe-yourself
2. https://www.artofwellbeing.com/2017/02/25/personal-qualities/
3. https://www.positivelypresent.com/2016/02/find-the-good-in-yourself.html

EXERCISE: AH-HA! AND UH-OH! FOUR

Reflect on the What are your Qualities? Exercise. As this list is somewhat similar to the Who are you Exercise, consider the same questions: Where did the rankings for today and the rankings for the future intersect? Were there rankings on one list that were close to rankings on the other list? For example, number 18 on your ranking for today was number 20 on your ranking for the future. Where did they diverge? Were there rankings that were from the extremeness that swapped? For example, an item near the end of your ranking for today is near the top of your ranking for the future (or vis versa).

Write for at least 10 minutes for the Ah-has, and 10 minutes for the Uh-ohs. You can simply make bullet points. You aren't writing poetry. Your insights are for you and need to only be easily recorded and easily accessible

EXERCISE – WHOM DO YOU ADMIRE?

You might be. Simply make a list of 10 people you admire. Then write a short paragraph on why you admire them. It is that easy (and that hard).

Now you may be stuck looking around you coming up with people you admire. Here are some guidelines that may help. You don't have to know them intimately. You can admire someone that you have never met or don't know in depth.

They don't have to be alive. It could be someone from your past or someone from history.

They don't have to be real. They could be a comic book character or someone from a book or movie who stood out to you for one reason or the next.

The important thing for each is that you dive deeply into why you admire them. And (at the risk of overstating), strive to avoid the generic or broad descriptions. For example. "I admire Fred because he is a cool guy and he is good and a lot of fun."

Top Three Resources for Whom to you Admire?
1. https://www.lifeuncivilized.com/who-do-you-admire/
2. https://www.psychologytoday.com/us/blog/putting-psyche-back-psychotherapy/201708/why-what-i-admire-in-you-also-says-something-about-me

3. https://www.theemotionmachine.com/role-models-make-a-list-of-people-you-admire-and-why/

EXERCISE: AH-HA! AND UH-OH! FIVE

Take a moment and review those people whom you admire. Do you notice anything that stands out between these people? Do you notice some similarities between the qualities you identified in the previous exercise and the people you admire? Do you see any qualities you missed in the previous exercise that you consider important to include?

Write for at least 10 minutes for the Ah-has and 10 minutes for the Uh-ohs.

WRAPPING IT ALL UP

You now have a total of five reflective journal entries (the Ah-has and Uh-ohs). You have explored the "shoulds" that are fired at you from a variety of sources. You have envisioned your perfect life, how you identify yourself, qualities that are key to who you are, and why you admire the people you admire.

And you have taken a hard look at the propaganda you are sold. Propaganda from the LGBTQIAPKers. Propaganda from the androphile community.

Now what? It is time to bring it all together in one piece that describes your vision (not your goals – those are not your vision) of who you are, the kind of person you strive to be, and the values you live your life by – your roadmap to your life.

But before you write that, take a moment and reflect upon these questions:

- How do I fit with the LGBTQIAPKers? I might have sex with men, but am I even gay – at less gay in the way that the propaganda, group-think leaders identify as gay?
- What does it mean to be an androphile?

Now, with the answers to these two questions in mind, get out your journal and write the following heading at the top of the page: "I am a man who is attracted to other men and I believe…"

Give yourself time to fill the page (or more) with your values and beliefs. Pay particular attention to addressing those tenants professed by the gay and androphile leaders. Get clarity on where you align and diverge from the propaganda put forth by these people. This is your "what."

When you are done, on the top of the next available page, write the following heading: "I am a man who is attracted to other men, and the life I live is…"

Give yourself time to fill the page (or more) with the actions you take in your life, the groups you interact with, and the hobbies and activities you pursue for fun and relaxation. Once again, pay particular attention to addressing those tenants professed by the gay and androphile leaders. Get clarity on where you align and diverge from their propaganda. This is your "how."

When you are done, on the top of the next available page write the following heading: "I am a man who is attracted to other men and my purpose is…"

Give yourself time to fill the page (or more) with the legacy you hope to create: What does your life mean? What do you want people to remember once you are gone? And, just like the previous two writing activities, pay attention to the propaganda. This is your "why."

Now what?
With your "what" and "how" and "why" in hand, you have set a trajectory that is about you and not some social movement's agenda. Talk about what you have learned with others who are fighting against the propaganda bullshit we are fed about what it means to be gay or androphile. Encourage others to do their own work. And if the political correctness police try to shut you down and accuse you of internalized homophobia, not being inclusive and shaming others, or any other unresolved issue, call them out, point out that they are the ones who are not being inclusive and shaming you, and tell them to shove their propaganda bullshit up their ass.

Extra Help

Are you stuck? Need extra help? I am happy to do a free 30-minute coaching session with you. HOWEVER, you must share with me (via email, Evernote, Google Docs, Dropbox, etc.) your responses to all the exercises, plus answer to these two questions: (1) why do you think you are stuck? (2) how would you have to be different to get unstuck easily?

You just can't message me, not do any work, and expect me to help you through whatever it is that you need help through. It's free to those who choose to do the work. Your effort is your payment not only to me but to yourself, and the dividends you collect from the investment of your time will pay off significantly during your coaching session.

Top Three Resources for Wrapping it Up
1. https://www.lifehack.org/499949/5-tips-for-making-your-own-path-in-life
2. https://www.suitedmonk.com/how-to-find-your-path-in-life/
3. https://thriveglobal.com/stories/why-is-it-important-to-follow-your-own-path/

AFTERWORD
You are NOT Someone Else's Political Pawn

"There are types of people who want to have leverage over other people's lives, for no other reason than they feel the need to have leverage. I find this to be a certain type of sickness of the mind. You could argue that they wish you no harm. However, the desire to simply have leverage over another—whether this is mental, emotional or physical —is, I think, a sickness of the mind. I can honestly say right now that I, 100%, have no manipulative intentions to gain leverage over any other person that I know."
— C. JoyBell C.

PRESSURE & CONFORMITY: WHAT IS IT REALLY ALL ABOUT?

You might be asking yourself, why all this pressure to be one way or another? Why is it an issue if I don't want to put on a pair of tight rainbow shorts, apply mascara, get drunk and sing off key to some remix of "I Am What I Am" from the musical La Cage aux Folles? What difference does it make? And, in the same sense, why is it an issue if I don't support abortion? And why is it an issue if I don't follow the other extreme and embrace the racist misogynist views put out by the original thinkers of the Androphile Movement?

I'll tell you why. It's all about money, specifically to which causes you donate. And it's all about your political actions, specifically what you do at the voting booth and whether or not you join some new "march on Washington" event.

Lots of money.

Endless political manipulation.

When you take actions to understand and develop your own self, including your own views, perspectives, goals, vision, and purpose, you are a threat to the armies of the left and the armies of the right who want you to join their platform in lockstep precision.

When you take these actions of self-development, you benefit only the army of yourself.

I hope this book has helped you take steps in that direction.

Whether you are now firmly seated in your view that you are not some fag with a gay pride flag stuck up his ass prancing around in the streets on some Saturday in June, or your view that you love your feminine side and would never dare go out in public without your eyeliner on, I hope the person you are embracing is who you truly are and not what someone else -- with some manipulative political agenda -- tells you who you are.

I hope I have ignited your journey, and I want to hear about it.

Don't Walk Away from Anything. Run Toward Your True Self

Unlike charlatans like Brandon Straka (https://www.walkawaycampaign.com), I am not telling you to walk away from the left. Brandon Straka is playing you just like the initial androphiles were. And they themselves are being played.

I did not write this book to play you. I wrote this book for you to play you. I wrote this book to empower your insight and your choices.

Similarly, I did not write this book to get you to walk away from one political movement only so you can be persuaded to walk into some other political movement. I wrote this book so you can explore and identify your own values, your own perspective, your own insights -- who you are at your core. I want you to clearly identify that and I want you to walk toward that. No strike that. I want you to <u>run</u> toward that.

COACHING, ABSOLUTELY FREE (KIND-OF)

I am so committed to wanting you to find self-empowerment, I am so committed to you getting out from under the political-correct hold of the LGBTQIAPKers , I am so committed wanting you to take action toward being the best androphile man that you can be, that I want to offer you a free coaching session to help you accelerate your progress.

Yep, it's free (kind of).

"Kind of" references the price of admission you must make in order to receive your coaching. You have to do some work – you have to complete all the exercises in this book.

Email your responses to me and I will reply with options for scheduling a 45-minute coaching session.

We'll connect on the phone just like to do with all my clients.

We'll debrief your learnings and insights from writings.

We'll work out a road map for your next steps.

I look forward to hearing from you.

All the best,

G. Scott Graham-Stephens

ABOUT SCOTT GRAHAM

Scott is a business and career coach from Boston, MA. When he is not coaching people to be their best, he participates in Tough Mudders, hikes, works on a farm, practices Vipassana meditation, and volunteers as an EMT and firefighter.

BOOKS BY SCOTT GRAHAM

Ten Things You Need to Know About Coaching Before You Get a Coach

Motivational Interviewing Made Easy

Work Exchange: A Handbook for Hosts

How to Become More Linkable... ...and Likeable on LinkedIn

Check! Your Guide to Creating a Life Transforming Bucket List

Growing & Using Good King Henry

Make Time Your Superhero Power!

Get Off Your Ass & Mow The Grass!

Now what? After Your Vipassana Course Is Over

Determining Marijuana Use in the Age of Legalization

Androphile Pride

Treatment Planning 101

CONTACT SCOTT GRAHAM

True Azimuth, LLC
265 Franklin Street
Suite 1702
Boston, MA 02110

Phone: (617) 475-0081

Website: http://TrueAzimuth.biz

Email: sgraham@TrueAzimuth.biz

Skype: TrueAzimuth

Twitter: @TrueAzimuth

Goodreads: https://www.goodreads.com/grahamgscott

Facebook: http://www.facebook.com/trueazimuthcoaching

LinkedIn: http://www.linkedin.com/company/true-azimuth-llc

ABOUT SUSAN WILLIAMS

Susan is a substance abuse counselor and copy editor in Bellows Falls, VT where she strives to live a self-sufficient, minimalist life. She has collaborated with Scott on a number of projects and completed hiking the 272-mile Long Trail with him in 2015. In 2021 Susan plans to accompany Scott as they tackle the 268-mile Pennine Way in the United Kingdom.

OTHER BOOKS BY SUSAN WILLIAMS

Determining Marijuana Use in the Age of Legalization